Printed in Great Britain
by Amazon

29574720R00059